Don't Miss Your Miracle

Don't Miss Your Miracle

Vance Havner

BAKER BOOK HOUSE
Grand Rapids, Michigan 49506

Copyright 1984 by
Baker Book House Company

ISBN: 0-8010-4280-1

First printing, May 1984
Second printing, January 1985

Printed in the United States of America

Contents

    Foreword   5
1. Don't Miss Your Miracle   7
2. Gideon's Fleece   8
3. A Way to Hell from the Gates of Heaven   9
4. God Knows Who's Who   10
5. Just Plain Vanilla   12
6. Stray Donkeys and Old Barns   13
7. Preacher Who Won't Quit   14
8. Bye, Bye, Robin   15
9. All for the Birds   16
10. Open Windows   17
11. More Open Windows   18
12. Faith Is More than Imagination   19
13. A Prophet Besides   20
14. Waterproofed Worship   21
15. Rubbish   22
16. All and Nothing   23
17. "Don't Demean Ye"   24
18. When Jesus Took a Nap   25
19. Foretaste of Glory   26
20. Moaning at the Bar   27
21. Babel, Babble, and Babylon   29
22. A Long Time Till Spring   31
23. "Except Ye Repent"   32
24. Signs of the Times   33
25. "And Knew Not"   34
26. Changing Deck Chairs on a Sinking Titanic   35
27. Silencing the Prophet   36
28. Wits' End—a Good Place to Start Over   38
29. When Jesus Came   39
30. So Near and Yet So Far   40
31. "Us" and "Them"   41
32. Nesting and Resting   42
33. The Big Buzzard Roost   43

34. "All Live Unto Him"   44
35. At Christmas Time   45
36. The Missing Love   46
37. Mr. Fearing   47
38. Motto on the Wall   48
39. When We Don't Know What to Do   49
40. A Sweet Little Girl   50
41. Two Ways to Leave Church   51
42. "Go, Tell That Fox"   52
43. Getting Used to It   53
44. Prison Birds at Midnight   54
45. Birds and Buses   55
46. "Tentative" and "Terminal"   56
47. The Ancient Sacrifice   57
48. "Only Believe"   58
49. Between Two Fires   59
50. Too Much   60
51. The Prevenient Angel   61
52. The Revival–Evangelism Mix-up   62
53. Bringing Back the King   63
54. Lord of the Leftovers   64
55. No More Sea   65
56. The Seventh Dip   69
57. Don't Pitch Toward Sodom!   70
58. The Attending Imediment   71
59. From Limp to Leap   72
60. Praying "Accordingly"   73

Foreword

Most of us do not read long articles and sermons these days, so these meditations are of the capsule variety. I wrote them in my eighty-first year and with an overloaded preaching schedule. They are for harassed and hurried souls when "Take Time to Be Holy" is an outdated hymn. Who has time to be holy? And yet time is one thing it takes. Our Lord rose up a great while before day and departed into a solitary place to pray. Was it William Law who said, "Who am I to lie folded up in a bed late in the morning while farmers are already about their work and I am so far behind with my sanctification?"

I am grateful to my Christian friend Beauford Smith for painstakingly typing the manuscript.

Vance Havner

1 Don't Miss Your Miracle

We often hear it said that the day of miracles is past. But every true Christian is a miracle, born again by the Holy Spirit. Of course I mean real Christians, not just church members. If you are what you have always been you are not a Christian. The Christian life is a miracle, Jesus living within the true believer. He is not just our Saviour and Lord but also our Life.

God has many miraculous things for His people, but so many miss them. I do not know what Jesus had for the rich young ruler, but he missed it. The blind man would have missed receiving his sight if he had not washed in Siloam. Demas missed his miracle when he deserted Paul. Jonah almost missed his life mission. I have met many who were called to preach or to be missionaries who never answered. My father was called to preach but never did and lived to regret it the rest of his life. I almost missed my miracle at one time. We live doing what comes naturally and miss what comes supernaturally.

Have you missed the miracle God had for you? So many live on crackers and cheese when they have a standing invitation to the banquets of God. But there may still be time for a miracle.

> "Down in the human heart crushed by the Tempter,
> Feelings lie buried that grace may restore;
> Touched by a loving heart, wakened by kindness,
> Chords that were broken may vibrate once more."

The church is a miracle. Today too many of its members are not miraculous but make-believe. Gideon asked, "Where be all his miracles which our fathers told us of?" (Judg. 6:13). Have you missed yours?

2 Gideon's Fleece

Gideon was no genius nor did he possess training or unusual faculties, but as he beat out grain on a threshing floor he remembered the great days of Israel's past and asked, "Where are the miracles today?" (cf. Judg. 6:13). At least he cared. There is far more hope for souls that grieved over the times than for the popular happiness boys. Gideon did not know a miracle when he saw one, as when the angel of God visited him. But God called him to leadership and gave him the sign of the fleece.

I have not been able to relate many experiences bordering on the miraculous. I have heard others who can, and I do not doubt the possibility, although some of the stories grow with the telling. I do remember the incident related in my book *Hope Thou in God* when I was low in spirits away from home and troubled about a sick wife who was quite ill and later died. I put down my bag in a lonely motel room where a Gideon Bible lay open on the table. It was opened to Psalms 42 and 43 where the words, "Why art thou cast down, O my soul? and why art thou disquieted within me? hope thou in God" are found three times without turning a page (42:5, 11; 43:5). I was assured that I would yet praise Him, and I do. I know that one cannot flip open a Bible every time and land on such a timely verse. In a time of great need one may find himself flipping to the details of the Tabernacle or the genealogies! But our Father often gives us a sign of the fleece when we are willing to do what follows.

You may be beating grain on a threshing floor, grieved over the times and wondering where God and His miracles are, but that is better than not expecting miracles at all.

3 A Way to Hell from the Gates of Heaven

Almost inside the kingdom of God but still outside: John Bunyan saw this awful possibility and wrote about it in *Pilgrim's Progress*. The thought is frightening.

Samuel Rutherford used to list such celebrities as Balaam, Pharaoh, Simon Magus, Caiaphas, Jehu, and Herod, as well as many others who had foretastes of glory yet rejected God.

One may know the Scriptures, believe sound doctrine, belong to a church, preach, prophesy, cast out demons, yet still go to hell.

This fearful possibility makes a Sunday morning congregation of church goers a mission field, since perhaps half or more have joined a church without knowing Jesus Christ. Only God knows who is who, but we true Christians have reason to suspect that we are outnumbered by our own members, and we cannot reach our goals because of the interference of our own team. Fearless preaching that calls the righteous to repentance is in order.

Bunyan was right. There is a way to hell from the gates of heaven!

4 God Knows Who's Who

Have you ever thought what your reaction might have been had you been present long ago when Jesus introduced His twelve disciples to the public? The most important movement of all time was beginning, and these men were the first gospel team in history. Surely our Lord would select outstanding specimens of manhood—educated, gifted in body, mind, and soul above the common run of humanity!

But who were these yokels fresh from fishing, from tax collecting for Rome, from political fanaticism? Surely Simon Peter was not the best material available! Nearly everything he said in the Gospels was a mistake! "We have left all to follow thee.... What shall we have therefore?" "Let us build here three tabernacles." "Thou shalt never wash my feet." "Lord, this shall never happen to thee." "Thou seest the crowd thronging thee and why askest thou, who touched me?" And then, horror of horrors, on that awful night of his Lord's trial, he cursed and swore that he never knew Jesus! Was this the best prospect available to lead the team of Twelve?

Among the Twelve were three other fishermen, Andrew, James, and John; Matthew, a Jewish tax collector for Rome; Simon Zelotes, a political enthusiast. And our Lord Himself once said to this dozen, speaking of Judas Iscariot, "Have not I chosen you and one of you is a devil?"

This just doesn't add up! Why didn't Jesus convert twelve Rabbis, familiar with the Scriptures, men of religion, of learning, of special abilities? What hope could there be for the gospel with a start like this?

Down through the centuries God has often dumbfounded us by the D. L. Moodys and Billy Sundays He has raised up above thousands of more promising prospects to win the multitudes to Him. Surely He is a

God of infinite surprises, raising up nonentities to identities and confounding all the experts.

But, to keep the record straight, our Lord made a breathtaking exception and picked a Pharisee of Pharisees from the school of Gamaliel, who knew the Scriptures. And yet, that strange Saul of Tarsus had blazed with a bitter hatred of Christ and had put to death the first believers. He had taken off on Damascus road, exhaling threats and slaughter. No ordinary conversion would ever stop such a devil-possessed man. So the Lord knocked him down, blinded him, and called him to be the greatest gospel preacher of all time.

But God selects some of all strata whether fishermen or fanatics, but not many wise, mighty, and noble, so that no flesh should glory in His presence.

Nowadays many young preachers or students expecting to preach come to see me. I love these boys, but I have quit long ago deciding who will be a great preacher! In 1938 I met a young man who welcomed me to the school he was attending and carried my bag into the building. I didn't know I had just met the boy who would preach to more people than any other preacher in history. But I have given up making personal judgments as to who is the likeliest candidate. I have been fooled both ways! God is sovereign, and we never know what He will do. I am glad He doesn't consult us!

5 Just Plain Vanilla

A Florida friend of mine, not a flashy, but a faithful Christian, said to me once, "I've never had many dramatic spiritual experiences. I guess you'd say I'm just plain vanilla."

The ice cream business dazzles us with fancy new flavors and new creations smothered in nuts and goo. Once in a while I try a new flavor, but I'll settle for plain vanilla as a day-by-day old friend.

There are all sorts of Christians depending on temperament, experience, and other factors. They can tell you of trips to third heaven or being cured of their thorn in the flesh, but I like best the day-by-day saint who is weak but strong in God's sufficient grace.

In years past I devoured books relating amazing dreams and visions and thrills of more favored saints. I sat up late in my room in the old St. John Hotel in Charleston, South Carolina, reading *Deeper Experiences of Great Christians*, trying to duplicate their stories. I have heard pulpit spell-binders tell dramatic stories and sometimes they added new features from time to time. The years have passed and many are gone, but now that I am past my eighty-first milestone, I'm just plain vanilla. And my favorite song is "Trusting Jesus, That Is All." I find that those who ply their daily task with busier feet are those whose secret souls a holier strain repeat, and most of them are plain vanilla.

The population of heaven is going to run high statistics on vanilla Christians. Churches couldn't operate without them. Thank God for the spectacular comets who sometimes flash across the sky, but hallelujah for the little stars who are there every night and who shine best when the sky is darkest!

6 Stray Donkeys and Old Barns

The first time we encounter Saul, King of Israel, he is on a mission from his father to locate stray donkeys. A man chosen to be a leader of God's people is on an unimportant side-trip that keeps him busy until he meets Samuel, who advises him, "Stop worrying about the donkeys. They have been found. Get going on your main business of being a king."

Many a servant of the Lord never gets his main work done because he fritters away time looking for runaway donkeys. Many a man called to be a preacher wears out in trivial missions, not necessarily evil, but not worth his time and effort. It is important to get our priorities in place.

I remember hearing a former pastor of mine tell about an art student sent by his teacher to paint a beautiful sunset. Within that scene stood an old barn. The artist spent the whole afternoon painting that old barn and as the sun was sinking the teacher came to see how things were going. In his amazement he cried, "I sent you to paint a sunset and you have spent all this time putting a roof on a barn!"

Are you spending your life painting barns instead of sunsets, looking for stray donkeys instead of carrying out the duties of a king? "They which receive abundance of grace and of the gift of righteousness shall reign in life by one, Jesus Christ" (Rom. 5:17). That is worth giving our lives to, leaving stray donkeys to those who seek nothing else. We must be about our kingly business!

7 Preacher Who Won't Quit

As I walked along the other day, a friend stopped mowing grass long enough to greet me. He called to a neighbor, "Come and meet a preacher who won't stop." I asked him, "Do you mean I preach too long?" Oh no, he meant that even though I am past eighty, I keep on preaching. Ministers these days terminate their work by retiring, doing supply or interim preaching, but I'm still a traveling minister most of the time. I began at twelve, and when one has been at it that long, preaching is not a profession but a lifestyle.

I'll never forget the day I stood in old Corinth Baptist Church and asked those dear farmer folk to license me to preach. I was scared half to death, but they did it. I never knew the day when I did not feel that I should be a preacher. God did not call me to preach only until age sixty-five. He left it open-ended. No preacher has a right to terminate his preaching.

Preaching is not like law or medicine or engineering or anything else on earth. It involves God saying, "Whom shall I send and who will go for us?" and a surrendered man saying, "Here am I, Lord, send me." One doesn't casually decide to take up preaching. It involves almighty God, the souls of men, heaven and hell—eternal issues that we can't play games with.

I have known men called to preach who never preached (my father was one), and others who gave up their calling. They are a sad lot.

For a few years I had a cold heart and wasted precious time. Those years might have been saved if I had run into some down-to-earth, rousing preaching that would have awakened me from my ease, but it was hard to find. The day when Dr. R. A. Torrey said to me, "Young man, make up your mind on one thing and stay with it," started something. He wasn't playing games! He would have me become a sword with one point and not a broom with straws pointing in all directions.

8 Bye, Bye, Robin

As I write, it is still mid-summer, but already there are signs that the melancholy days will soon be here, the saddest of the year. The cicadas have struck up their strident welcome to autumn, and the wood thrush is silent. The robins are still plentiful, but already I anticipate their retirement, muttering under my breath, "Mr. Robin, I'll be missing you."

I know what it means in early spring to see the first arrivals. Mr. Robin is such a gentleman among the birds. His "Cheerily, cherrup" sees Old Man Winter out and ushers in the early blossoms. No matter how cold the winds have been, how fiercely the chilling blasts have blown, all is forgotten in the new burst of coming spring—the robins are back!

We begin to feel that if by now we have endured the flu and the barren woods and put up with all our cold weather wraps, life is worth living again because we are on the threshold of another spring. Spring means a resurrection, a new beginning, a fresh start. The robins never fail to return! April always makes it, though sometimes with a late snowfall. More certain than the way it looks some days, the calendar wins; and "when the red, red robin comes bob, bob, bobbin' along," we take fresh heart. Likewise, when we long for departed dear ones, the robin reminds us that there is no final farewell—Christians never meet for the last time!

15

9 All for the Birds

I have been reading an account of the life of John James Audubon, the greatest artist-naturalist of the United States, master painter of *The Birds of America*, and master ornithologist. He was without formal learning, a wanderer over the earth, almost obsessed by his love for birds and a passion to make them better known. No hardship or hindrance kept him from his goal, and he reached it. We now have Audubon clubs and his name appears on many a spot dedicated to the cause of ornithology.

One thinks of devotees to other causes—some less worthy—men and women spending their lives in utter abandon, disregarding pain and persecution for a cause. Peter and John, fresh from seeing the risen Christ, fresh from Pentecost, make their debut in Acts 3 as evangelists of the gospel, sold out to Jesus Christ. One would die a violent death, the other end up an exile on lonely Patmos. Nothing mattered but Jesus, to know Him and to make Him known.

Alexander MacLaren was right in saying that Christianity has fallen into the hands of a church that does not half believe its own gospel. Glorious exceptions there are, thank God, but the average church member singing, "To the old rugged cross I will ever be true, its shame and reproach gladly bear," is anything but a martyr. Peter and John were so devoted to Jesus that miracle power was theirs. They aroused an amazed world and received a storm of opposition from organized religion. Two lowly fishermen, by knowing that Name above every name and the power behind it, saw miracles happen. And well might we sing, "Ye blind, behold your Saviour come and leap ye lame for joy" and see crippled souls changed from limping to leaping if we were as all out for Jesus as was Audubon for the birds.

10 Open Windows

Daniel is one of the greatest characters in the Bible. A Hebrew, he rose to prominence in a foreign empire and was admired and promoted by a pagan monarch, yet he never wavered from his faith in God. Daniel maintained his integrity against all the wiles and wickedness of heathen Babylon. In his bedroom he kept windows open toward Jerusalem. To Daniel Jerusalem spoke of God and His faithfulness, and his enemies found no grounds to accuse him except concerning his religion. On that point he never wavered and on that score he speaks to every true Christian living in this heathen age. He kept his windows open toward Jerusalem!

In this hour the downlook is hideous and the outlook is frightening. But the uplook is as good as ever if the windows are open. The tragedy of these days is that so many Christians have closed their windows toward heaven. Many do not believe in a miracle-working God who still intervenes in the affairs of men and particularly in the cause of His servants. Many carry on religious activities as though heaven has gone out of business and as though God does not interfere with the course of things. Some hold so-called revivals, but it is evident that they do not expect any breakthroughs from heaven.

I have read of a time when drought struck hard, crops died, streams dried up, and finally in desperation one farming area called the people to assemble at church and pray for rain. Many responded, but it was observed that only one little girl brought an umbrella! She said, "We are going to ask God for rain and when it comes we will need umbrellas!" But nobody else really looked for showers of blessing.

Unless Christians and churches reopen their windows toward Jerusalem for the unusual and unscheduled invasion of God in His own way, the forums and committee meetings and programs mean nothing. "All is vain unless the Spirit of the Holy One come down." Is your window open toward Jerusalem?

11 More Open Windows

Open windows toward heaven is only part of a two-way experience. Speaking of our tithes and gifts to God, we read His promise: "Prove me now herewith, if I will not open you the windows of heaven and pour you out a blessing, that there shall not be room enough to receive it" (Mal. 3:10). This means generous giving, not a measly dollar on a collection plate by a tightwad who feels like singing as he gives it, "When we asunder part, it gives us inward pain." It is more like the little boy who had no money to give but slipped into the collection plate a paper bearing the words, "I give myself." God doesn't want your money if He doesn't have you. "Self, service, substance" is the proper order.

You cannot outgive God. Giving is not meant to be a way to get rich quick, but God does repay a thousand times over the one who gives with no strings attached. Paul wrote of having nothing and yet possessing all things. Satan cannot do much with that kind of Christian. He cannot give him anything for he has everything, nor can he take away because he has nothing!

Keep your windows open toward heaven and God will open heaven's blessings to you. "Give, and it shall be given unto you; good measure, pressed down, and shaken together, and running over" (Luke 6:38).

Try it and prove it! Get on the giving side with God. Be like Daniel with his window open toward Jerusalem.

12 Faith Is More than Imagination

Paul said, "Christ liveth in me" (Gal. 2:20). A Christian is indwelt by the living Lord. This is a glorious fact, but many Christians have trouble making it real. How do we become aware of Christ's presence? Too many confuse faith with imagining He lives within us and trying to act as though it were true. Faith is not a sort of holy imagination. Jesus lives within any heart where He has been invited to abide. It may not always feel or look like it, but the certainty of His indwelling does not rest upon any one mood whether it be good or bad. We have His word for it. Christ said if we opened our heart's door and invited Him in He would do so. He must of course come in as the guest and take over as the host. But it is no mere theological possibility—He is there! We are to live not as though He lives in us, but because He is in us we should live accordingly.

Christ made it crystal clear: "He that hath my commandments, and keepeth them, he it is that loveth me: and he that loveth me shall be loved of my Father, and I will love him, and will manifest myself to him" (John 14:21). Christ makes Himself real to the obedient believer and disciple.

Do not wait for rare thrills and special happenings. These may come, but the key is obedience. "If ye know these things, happy are ye if ye do them" (John 13:17). There is no other way to be happy in Jesus but to trust and obey. The key is not imagination or imitation, but obedience to His Word and will. Finney said, "A revival is a new beginning of obedience to God." We are awfully short of that kind of revival—individually and congregationally today! New Testament Christianity is being what we are by the indwelling Christ.

13 A Prophet Besides

When good King Jehoshaphat went into partnership with wicked Ahab against Ramoth-gilead, he proposed that the clergy be invited to give their counsel. They approved the project, but Jehoshaphat was not convinced and asked, "Is there not here a prophet of the Lord besides, that we might enquire of him?" (1 Kings 22:7). Ahab replied, "There is . . . one . . . but I hate him; for he doth not prophesy good concerning me, but evil" (v. 8). In John 7:7 we read that Jesus' brothers advised Him to handle His publicity better and go up to Jerusalem to perform His wonderful works. He replied, The world hates me, "because I testify of it, that the works thereof are evil."

You will observe that Micaiah and our Lord were not fair weather prophets, they gave evil times a bad name. Today any preacher who says the days are evil is accused of being a pessimist. One would have to be blind in both eyes and bereft of his brains not to see these days as evil, yet the happy boys are always painting the clouds with sunshine when the Scriptures hold no such view of things as they are. They envisage a redeemed earth and a returning King, but our business now is to redeem the time because the days are evil.

In a day when the four hundred bade Ahab and Jehoshaphat go up against Ramoth-gilead and prosper, it is not easy to be "a prophet besides." He may fare, as did Micaiah, on bread and water for being the oddball, but he follows in the footsteps of the Son of God whom the world hated because He said the days were evil.

14 Waterproofed Worship

The great English preacher, Alexander Maclaren, did not take lightly the indifference of some of his congregation and did not fail to say so. Once he lamented, "You do not know the despair that comes over us preachers time after time, as we look down upon the faces of our congregations and feel, "What shall I do to put a sharp enough point upon this truth to get it into the heart of some man who has been sitting there as long as I have been standing here, and is never a bit the better for it?" He said, "Some of you have been listening, listening, listening, until your systems have become so habituated to this Christian preaching that it does not produce the least effect. It all runs off you like rain off waterproof."

In other words, today we would say "like water off a duck's back." Waterproofed worship! Maclaren also said that a man can live by the side of Niagara until he cannot hear the cataract! It is a frightening thought that a church goer can immunize himself against the truth by continually hearing it without receiving it. The Scriptures tell of those who hearing hear not. At church some turn off the hearing aids God gave them and might as well have them in their pockets during the sermon. It is a sad day for the preacher who accepts such conditions and suffers none of Maclaren's anguish about it.

That businessman present in body but absent in mind, that elegant lady with thoughts a thousand miles removed from church, ought not be merely accepted as a matter of course with nothing to be done about it. Maclaren said that it is better that they go out displeased than that they just go out. The issues of life and death, heaven and hell, are too urgent to be waterproofed out by mere indifference.

15 Rubbish

The rebuilders of the wall of Jerusalem grew tired and discouraged, saying, "The strength of the bearers of burdens is decayed, and there is much rubbish; so that we are not able to build the wall" (Neh. 4:10). Any construction site has rubbish. Sometimes the odds and ends, the broken pieces, the bricks and stones lie crushed, and junk accumulates until the exhausted workers feel like throwing up their hands and giving up the whole project. Beautiful buildings stand at one stage amidst what looks like the wreckage of a dream, instead of a thing of loveliness soon to rise out of all the debris. It is at such a point in the process that weariness almost stops the enterprise.

Christians have periods when there seems to be nothing but rubbish in their lives. Broken dreams, failures in judgment, tiredness of the flesh, or the scorn of the enemy almost drive the saint back to his sinning. The world looks on and laughs at the Christian who has set out to live a godly life, and the new testimony is not yet visible amid the broken efforts and smashed endeavors. Pastors have to deal with rubbish in the building of a New Testament church, in the midst of the skepticism and cynicism of these godless times.

We are imperfect human beings, and we will make blunders, and rubbish will accumulate. We should seek forgiveness and learn from our mistakes, but not let them beat us into overdoing our self-reproach so that it breaks our spirit. No saint ever lived who did not wrestle with rubbish. Either he lets it smother him, or he will rise to victory above it. Sanballat will sneer, and Satan will say that even a fox could tear up the edifice, as they said in the days of Nehemiah. But the day came when they carted off the rubbish and the wall stood as a monument to brave souls who "prayed and set a watch." Yes, even one-eyed praying is necessary sometimes, but it pays!

16 All and Nothing

Paul says of himself and others that as Christians we have nothing yet possess all things (1 Cor. 3:22; 2 Cor. 6:10). He enumerates what is ours: "Paul, or Apollos, or Cephas"—that is, all the preachers are ours. We are prone to identify with only one as "my preacher." Paul, Cephas, and Apollos were utterly different types, but Paul does not trumpet the superiority of his favorite. Paul also says that "the world," is ours. It will be under our sway one day, and the meek shall inherit the earth. The very "life" we live now is ours as is "death." We are not the victims of death. "Things present" and "things to come" are ours. What a shake-up of our terminology this means!

With such a situation, the devil may threaten to take away what we have; but we answer, "I have nothing." If he offers to give us this and that we say, "I have everything!" Not even the devil can do anything with a Christian like that!

The church today has all this wealth, but is rarely aware of it. Peter said to the lame man, "Silver and gold have I none; but such as I have give I thee: In the name of Jesus Christ of Nazareth rise up and walk" (Acts 3:6). The Pope said to Thomas Aquinas as they walked amid the splendor of the Vatican, "You can see that now the church cannot say, 'Silver and gold have I none.' " Aquinas replied, "True, but neither can she say, 'Rise and walk'!" Our huge and magnificent churches are well stocked with silver and gold. But the blind are not seeing, nor the lame walking in comparable numbers.

It is time for a new assessment of our spiritual arithmetic; we must get back to all and nothing!

17 "Don't Demean Ye"

Bobby Burns advises us in his inimitable way that if we have failed at some point, if "some hap mistake" has overtaken us, "yet still keep up a decent pride" and "Don't o'er far demean ye."

Of course when we sin we should confess our sins and forsake them and claim the cleansing blood of Christ. But we are not to demean and speak evil of ourselves in self-accusation. True humility does not think meanly of self; it does not think of self at all. Such self-demeaning souls worry us on one side and self-boasters irritate us on the other. Let us confess our sins to God and to each other if the occasion demands it, then move on as though it had not happened after we have learned our lesson from it. Some dear souls neither glorify God nor bless others by forever bemoaning past mistakes. Time is precious, and we waste a lot of it remembering and magnifying our past blunders.

Our Lord did not give Simon Peter a long discharge for denying Him but after the broken disciple reaffirmed, "Thou knowest I love thee," immediately set him to feeding lambs (John 21:15).

Don't let your bad day cast its evil spell over the rest of your life. "Don't o'er far demean ye."

18 When Jesus Took a Nap

We do not usually visualize our Lord in commonplace experiences, but He was human and sometimes tired, as when He slept in a boat on the Sea of Galilee after a long day of ministering. The wind can stir up plenty of trouble on the Sea of Galilee, and this tempest was quite a blast. The disciples had seen our Lord do many miracles, but how easily do we forget yesterday's deliverances when disaster threatens us today!

I remember hearing Dr. Clyde Francisco telling us that the First Adam had dominion over the birds of the air, the beasts of the field, and the fish of the sea; but he could not control wind or water. Sometimes we can bridle and use them, but they can turn on us and blow us away or drown us. But on the Sea of Galilee that day the Last Adam was in the boat, and what the First Adam could not master, the Last Adam could control!

The story ends with a glowing testimony: "What manner of man is this, that even the winds and the sea obey him!" (Matt. 8:27). If wind and water put you into a panic, and God seems to be taking a nap, don't ask, "Carest thou not that we perish?" Just make sure He is a passenger in your boat!

19 Foretaste of Glory

The writer of Hebrews tells us about those who "have tasted ... the powers of the world to come" (6:5). Our Lord came to bring in a kingdom of which He was the embodiment. It will be set up visibly when He returns to reign. Meanwhile, it is a spiritual kingdom of righteousness, peace, and joy in the Holy Spirit. Our Lord gave us samples of what the order of things to come will be like as He preached and healed among us. It is our privilege to taste of those joys in advance. Fanny Crosby said the assurance of salvation is a "foretaste of glory divine."

Years ago a fellow minister and I were preaching in a Bible conference. One night I preached on this theme. The other preacher and I rode to our hotel together. For a few moments we were silent. Then he suddenly burst into singing:

> "The hill of Zion yields a thousand sacred sweets
>   Before we reach the heavenly fields
>   Or walk the golden streets."

In other words, the trees of that fair land come to bend over the wall, and we can taste now a bit of their fruit! They offer a pledge of better things to come. In my boyhood days, book salesmen often left with us a prospectus, sample pages of the book; and it was frustrating to turn from page 25 to 42! The crumbs made me hungry for the cake. Likewise, in joy of Bible study, fellowship with other Christians, delights of prayer, refreshment of worship we only taste the powers of the age to come. We live on specimens of the fruit from Canaan without yet possessing the land that is still to be ours. Let us enjoy the snacks until we get to the big supper, the foretaste before we reach the feast!

20 Moaning at the Bar

"Sunset and evening star,
And one clear call for me!
And may there be no moaning at the bar,
When I put out to sea."

Between the years 1919 and 1925 three great Americans crossed the bar, and the circumstances were mournful. They had scaled great heights but passed away in sadness. First to go was Theodore Roosevelt, who drove himself at a furious pace, ending his White House years to hunt lions in Africa, running again for the presidency but missing it, and, at nearly sixty, exploring a Brazilian jungle. At last, sick and disappointed, blind in one eye and deaf in one ear, Roosevelt died in his sleep in his quiet home at Sagamore Hill. Broken in heart over the loss of his son Quentin, there was a moaning in his heart when he crossed the bar.

Woodrow Wilson passed away in 1924. At his peak he rode through throngs here and abroad, the foremost citizen of that short time, only to die with broken body and heart crushed over the failure of his efforts to launch the League of Nations.

William Jennings Bryan, America's greatest orator, three-time candidate for the presidency but never a winner, died in 1925. Harry Truman said, "I never heard another voice like the voice of Bryan." (I heard him four times myself!) But he died within a few days after his witness-stand confrontation with Clarence Darrow in the Scopes Monkey Trial. Today it is no tribute to America that men still applaud the infidel lawyer and scorn one of the finest Christians who ever held a Cabinet seat in Washington.

But there was another death beside which all others fade in relative insignificance. When the Son of God died on Calvary's hill it looked to some to be the greatest of all failures. His heart was broken indeed, but because of what really happened there it was the outstanding triumph of all history. The cross has been from that day not a sad symbol of failure, but the emblem of our only hope for forgiveness and the key to heaven. Paul said, "For me to live is Christ, and to die is gain" (Phil. 1:21). To be savingly identified with Him makes even death a paying proposition! And it guarantees no moaning at the bar when we put out to sea!

21 Babel, Babble, and Babylon

In the early days of history the human race began a Tower of Babel "that would reach to heaven." God overwhelmed that program with confusion of tongues. Through the centuries every time man has started a new tower to heaven God has smashed Babel with babble of one sort or another. Caesar and Charlemagne and Napoleon and Hitler and countless others have tried in vain to create new societies and new cultures and new empires that crashed in confusion. Egypt leaves its pyramids, Rome its Colosseum, Greece its Parthenon—Babels that ended in babble.

The Book of Revelation ends this string of Babels with the final Babylon. Eschatology has diverse schools of interpretation and never will they agree as to what this Babylon will be, where it will be, and what the future of it will be. I have read pages of the schools of thought and have not sold out to any of these prophets, but one would have to be blind in both eyes and bereft of brains not to see today the Babel of Babels being readied for the judgment of God.

The new humanism, in which man is fast becoming his own god, boasts the achievements of science in their application through industry to the creation of a larger life for all humankind. We see brainboggling achievements of inventive genius, view their application through industry, but look in vain for that larger life for all humankind. All we see is Babel and all we hear is babble.

We tremble at the horrors of nuclear destruction. We marvel at the rapid advances in computer technology. We sicken as we hear of herpes, the new curse of the sex insanity of our time. Bible eschatologists of the old school see an end-time world religion with Rome as its center. They believe that the commercial and industrial Babylon that rises in Revelation represents commerce, plagued by chaotic business deals, high taxes, and high oil prices.

The world's troubles head up one day in Antichrist, who has all the answers. The final clash between the God who became man and the man who will claim to be God draws nigh. One does not have to understand all the details to sum it up.

Scholars argue whether the church will go through the Great Tribulation. Whatever they think, tribulation beyond words is around us now—only a sample of what it will become. But our Lord will crush Babel and its babble in due time. Antichrist will have his fling, but he is doomed. My Bible has no devil on the first page and no devil on the last page! Babylon is not the last chapter!

In the days of the first Babylon Belshazzar put on a feast and all the notables attended. The prophet Daniel had not been given an invitation to sip ginger ale, crack jokes, and add a religious aura to the drunken orgy. The man of God who understands what God is writing on the wall can afford to wait until he is sent for. The feast of Babylon is being scheduled today. The last of the Babylons draws near. Blessed is the Daniel who can wait his time, who understands Babel, babble, and Babylon.

22 A Long Time Till Spring

As I write, it is early November, and I have been walking around the lake twice every day. The woods are at their autumn best, but everywhere one feels the mood of the season. The poet called these "the melancholy days, the saddest of the year." The falling leaves float down across my path. I am reminded of another poet's lines about himself as the last leaf on the bough made barren by the passing of so many old friends of bygone years. Well, at least autumn gradually conditions us for winter, else we might not withstand that onslaught. As far as I am concerned, the best part of winter is that it comes just before spring. I live for springtime, those few magic weeks so long in coming, so soon in departing.

The birds are few and mostly silent. Autumn finds only a remnant left to hold the fort until the robins sound the all-clear again. I saw some juncos, or snowbirds, as we used to call them. I welcome them for they will help cheer up a long winter. A mockingbird was singing valiantly a week ago, but the killer frost must have discouraged him. The best singer now is the white-throated sparrow with his high-pitched little melody that starts like "The Wedding March" upped several octaves. The nuthatches, chickadees, titmice, and woodpeckers will see winter through along with the flicker. Of course the blue jay will squawk for the duration. Squirrels are everywhere, bright-eyed and bushy-tailed, for this is their busiest season.

I suppose that autumn is the most fitting season for a man in his eighties. There remains only the winter of old age. Did I say "only"? Beyond winter lies eternal springtime. Heaven must be just that, for leaves will not fall nor flowers fade nor shall we wither and die. I will get enough springtime then for once and forever but never too much, for there can never be too much springtime for me here or hereafter. So, any way you look at it, in terms of a year or in terms of a lifetime, for the Christian, autumn is not too sad nor is even winter, for spring cannot be far behind.

23 "Except Ye Repent"

Alexander Whyte used to say something about the type of church listener who on Sunday morning is glad to have the preacher tell "when the Gospels were writ," or explain the meaning of Euroclydon or *Anathema Maranatha*; but who, if the minister dwells on such subjects as affects his living, cannot bear to be thus instructed. Was it Coleridge who spoke of those truths which are regarded as so true that they lose the power of truth and lie bedridden in the dormitory of the soul? And what about the pronouncement of Alexander Maclaren that "familiarity with Jesus Christ can be our ruin"?

The gospel often fares better with people who fight it than with people who trifle with it. G. Campbell Morgan said the church patronized is the church in peril and often paralyzed. Our Lord told the people of His hometown, Capernaum, that Sodom and Gomorrah would fare better in the judgment than the city that took Him for granted, that lived in the Light and paid no attention to it, that refused to repent.

No other gospel doctrine is more neglected today than is repentance. In the present self-centered generation old-fashioned conviction of sin is generally unheard of because sin is no longer sin. The new pulpit pitch is not geared to repentance. We bemoan the moral putridity of Sodom and well we may, but we had better weep over polite Capernaumites who wouldn't harm Jesus for anything but will never come to Him in repentance.

24 Signs of the Times

Some months ago the outbreak of the herpes epidemic brought *Time* magazine to make it the subject of their front cover. In another issue a computer was shown on the front cover as the recipient of the "Man of the Year" award. There is a strange bit of a letdown in honoring machines above their inventors. The whole drift these days is weird and uncanny. Man has come from secularism to humanism, and he is his own god. Morally he laughs at the law of God, but the herpes outbreak is the judgment of almighty God on humankind's collapse of moral law. The computer rash is another angle of the same story, which tells of a new generation of manikins in the offing.

The egghead apostles of the new progress have their untranslatable explanations, but God is not mocked. An old Book now smiled upon in lofty condescension by these blind leaders of the blind has spelled out the meaning of such signs and wonders and of our destiny.

Of course prophecy experts have had a field day in our time. They have come with diagrams and explanations as incomprehensible as those of the superscientists. Some of us do not favor any school of interpretation that goes to weird extremism. The prayer of my heart is that, like the children of Issachar in Bible days, I might have understanding of the times to know what Israel (and now all of God's people) ought to do.

No book is as up to date as the Bible. Do not lose your balance in the world's insanity. God is still on the throne and He knows what time it is.

25 "And Knew Not"

Jesus tells us that before the Flood people were eating and drinking, marrying and giving in marriage, selling, planting, building, "and knew not until the flood came" (Matt. 24:38-39). We are told that so shall it be when Jesus returns. Despite modern sophistication the primary characteristics of that generation will be ignorance—"they knew not."

Of the activities mentioned here not one is evil in itself, but when practiced without God all are worldly. This generation is utterly oblivious to the Word and will of God. Most people don't know that Jesus may come at any time and many probably wouldn't care if they did know. Preachers used to preach about selected sins and call them worldly, but those sins were only marks of the lifestyle of the times. Worse than certain popular sins is the awful ignorance of a generation that knows not the thing most worth knowing. Break into a conversation today and ask people if they are expecting Jesus to come back. That will bring a look that takes you for a nut! Indeed, most church members grow strangely silent and change the subject.

We have split the atom and have walked on the moon, and we quail at the possibility of nuclear disaster, but something greater still is not deemed worthy of discussion. After listing all the technical achievements of this generation will it be written at the end of their chapter, "They knew not"?

26 Changing Deck Chairs on a Sinking Titanic

Mordecai Ham used to say that the sinking of the Titanic in 1912 was God's object lesson to America, but we never learned it. Many ships have gone down, but that this "unsinkable" masterpiece of shipbuilding should go down on its first trip and that simply by encountering a massive hunk of ice, still seems uncanny—not just an accident but an event accompanied by strange and sinister circumstances that allow no explanation.

We are living in an hour when we seem to be on a toboggan slide out of control, worshipers of ourselves in the putridity of this age of humanism. "Judgment Day" and "end of the world" have disappeared from our vocabulary. The remedies for the world's troubles proposed by experts are pitiful. Recently I heard the observation that the remedies offered for our malignancy are about as sensible as changing the chairs on the deck of a sinking titanic!

One day each man has to face death whether he likes it or not. The Scriptures envision judgment day and heaven and hell. We have a date with destiny and an appointment with the Almighty. Every person has such an hour in God's book whether he has noted it or not. We could be nearing that time, and only faith in the Christ who believed it and taught it can save us.

Any effort to arrange for eternal life otherwise is like changing deck chairs on a sinking Titanic!

27 Silencing the Prophet

Prophets have never been plentiful, and the species is threatened with extinction. In other days Satan silenced prophets by slaughtering them. Our Lord reminded the Pharisees of the long list of God's spokesmen for whose demise their fathers were responsible. The tally has lengthened considerably since those days. Of course John the Baptist's head is not brought in on a platter in this generation. There are elegant modern ways of silencing prophets.

Some have been hushed up by promotion. The powers that be may elevate the prophet into a bishopric or give him a seat at headquarters, and he is never heard from again. Nothing will quench the spirit of an Elijah more effectively than to honor him in the courts of Ahab. John the Baptist was not a guest in Herod's palace. He was a prisoner in Herod's jail.

The prophet does not function well in official positions and is ill at ease on committees. He is suspicious of any moves to make him president of any ecclesiastical body. Once he assumes such a post a thousand subtle influences begin to bear upon him, and he is gradually reduced from a voice to an echo. When he represents a mixture he tries to speak for everybody and fails to speak for God. Prophets belong in the wilderness; they are easily smothered in an office.

When the prophet's ministry reaches such proportions that he has to be recognized even by those who dislike him, various devices may be employed to throttle down his volume and hamper his liberty. He may be assigned a devotional on the program to keep him from preaching. He may be given his subjects in advance to make sure he keeps within the limits of innocuous discourse. Some chairmen and emcees are noticeably nervous while he speaks and are immeasureably relieved when he finishes.

Some of his contemporaries in the prophets' school criticize him for saying what they would like to say if only they dared.

This world and many in the church are in conspiracy against prophets who refuse to be made over into priests. The pressure may intensify until Jeremiah is tempted to say, "I will not make mention of him, nor speak any more in his name." But the bone-fire within him is too hot for that. Between fire or forebearance that prophet chooses to burn. He may make the atmosphere uncomfortable for all lukewarm souls around him but better that than for all of them to sleep together. This tepid age can make false peace look so good and proper that any exception to the rule appears unchristian. To speak out in black and white when gray is the fashion is unforgivable. To break the pattern of what Joseph Parker called "middle zones, graded lines, light compounded with shadow in a graceful exercise of give and take," is the thankless task of that rare breed of prophet who will not be silenced.

28 Wits' End—a Good Place to Start Over

Wits' end is one of the most frequented stopping places on life's journey. We reach the end of our resources, our judgment, our calculations, and still no decision seems best or even good. It can be the fork of the road for either good or bad. King Jehoshaphat was at wits' end when he said, "We know not what to do," but he was on the way out when he added, "but our eyes are upon thee."

It may be declining health, shrinking finances, family trouble, the choice of a trade or profession—you name it—that brings us to our wits' end. The prodigal son came to wits' end when he came to himself as he fed the swine. He said, "I will arise and go to my father."

Wits' end is a good place to start, because our own wits are not so good anyway. We may acquire knowledge, but wisdom comes from God, and we get that when we ask for it in faith. When we are at the end of ourselves, there God begins. We must place ourselves in God's hands without reservation. We can expect an answer, maybe not what we want, but what glorifies Him.

If you are at your wits' end, cheer up. It is a great place to start over!

29 When Jesus Came

When Jesus came He made such an impact that all history is judged by its relation to Him. Celebrities have marched across the stage of history and made little difference, but by Jesus Christ all men are judged and their destiny determined. A man may make other poor decisions and be temporarily worse, but if he decides wrongly about Jesus Christ he is eternally worse.

One day a wicked woman started to a well in sin and shame. Then Jesus came and proved that He had the answer to her *depravity*. He turns the sordid to the sacred and bums into believers.

Another poor woman, dying of an incurable disease, health and money gone, awoke to what looked like a hopeless day. When Jesus came this poor soul touched Him while others only thronged Him and met the answer to *despair*.

A Gadarene demoniac, a wild man that chains couldn't bind and men couldn't tame met Jesus and found the answer to *demonism*.

Lazarus died but came to life when Jesus conquered *death*.

The risen Christ walked through a door without opening it to meet his sad disciples, and He lifted their discouragement.

Simon Peter denied his Lord but met Him at a fire on the beach and was delivered from *defeat*.

When Jesus comes our lives are changed. One day He will come again and clear up the *dilemma* of history.

> "When Jesus comes the tempters power is broken,
> When Jesus comes the tears are wiped away.
> He takes the gloom and fills the life with glory,
> For all is changed when Jesus comes to stay."

"Even so, come, Lord Jesus!"

30 So Near and Yet So Far

John Bunyan in *Pilgrim's Progress* perceived that "there was a way to hell, even from the gates of heaven." Jesus said to a scribe who had agreed with the two greatest commandments, "Thou art not far from the kingdom of God" (Mark 12:34). But a miss is as bad as a mile. One may know the Scriptures and yet not know Jesus. He said in essence, "You search the Scriptures but you will not come unto me." One may be as near as sound doctrine and miss Jesus. Martha believed in the resurrection, but she needed to move from the doctrinal to the personal. "I am the life," Jesus told her (John 11:25). One may call Him Lord and say one day, "We have prophesied and cast out demons in your name," only to hear Him say, "Depart, you workers of iniquity; I never knew you" (cf. Matt. 7:22, 23). One may be an enquirer, as was the rich young ruler, and never be a disciple.

Some are confused when they hear all this and then read that some of Jesus' disciples failed miserably, even to forsaking Him for the moment. Simon Peter was a disgrace to the cause he espoused on several occasions, but he had the root of the matter in him and loved his Lord. Old Mister Fearing in *Pilgrim's Progress* lived his life afraid he wouldn't get to heaven, but he got there anyway, because deep inside he trusted—though with a feeble faith.

It takes more than close proximity to the Lord to save us. Near is not close enough. Only simple faith, as of a little child, can save us.

31 "Us" and "Them"

In 1 Thessalonians 5:1-10 Paul is writing about two kinds of people. There are only two kinds of people on earth, Christians and everybody else. Throughout these verses these two kinds of people stand in absolutely different categories. There are no similarities; there are only contrasts.

When Paul is writing about Christians he says "we" and "us." When he means everybody else he says "they" and "them." Look at the contrast!

"But of the times and the seasons, brethren, *ye* have no need that I write unto *you*. For *yourselves* know perfectly that the day of the Lord so cometh as a thief in the night. For when *they* shall say, Peace and safety; then sudden destruction cometh upon *them*, as travail upon a woman with child; and *they* shall not escape. But *ye*, *brethren*, are not in darkness, that that day should overtake *you* as a thief. *Ye* are all the children of light, and the children of the day: *we* are not of the night, nor of darkness. Therefore let *us* not sleep as do *others*; but let *us* watch and be sober. For *they* that sleep sleep in the night; and *they* that be drunken are drunken in the night. But let *us*, who are of the day, be sober, putting on the breastplate of faith and love; and for an helmet, the hope of salvation. For God hath not appointed *us* to wrath but to obtain salvation by our Lord Jesus Christ, who died for *us*, that, whether *we* wake or sleep, *we* should live together with him" (italics mine).

Only two kinds of people. Jesus told us (John 17) that His followers have been saved out of this world, that we are still in it but not of it, that we have been saved to go right back into it to win others out of it—and that is the only business we have in it!

32 Nesting and Resting

The heart of man longs for a dwelling place. We sing, "Jesus, Lover of my soul, let me to Thy bosom fly," and "In the secret of His presence how my soul delights to hide!" The psalmist wrote about the sparrows and swallows that nested in God's Temple. Today God doesn't dwell in a temple, rather His Spirit dwells in men.

The psalmist wrote, "He that dwelleth in the secret place of the most High shall abide under the shadow of the Almighty" (91:1). We cannot *rest* in God until we *nest* in God. To nest is to settle, to abide. Some of us fly to God in a panic when we get into trouble and then wonder why we get so little comfort.

Augustine's mother wanted to go with him on a long trip. He feared that she was too old for such a trip, but she said, "My life is hid with Christ in God and when you are homed in God you cannot die away from home!" Nesting in God does not mean living the life of a hermit. The sparrow does not stay in the nest all the time, but goes back and forth about his business. He is based, however, and is rested because he is nested.

But do not look for an abiding peace if you are not abiding. Do not expect to rest until you first have nested and settled down in God. Make Him your permanent address, not a place to run to only when you get in a jam. You can't really rest until you really nest.

33 The Big Buzzard Roost

"Wheresoever the carcase is, there will the vultures be gathered together" (Matt. 24:28).

Never in the history of the earth has there been such a crop of slain carcases from the ravages of drugs and liquor, crime, and sex diseases.

When Jesus was born in Bethlehem Herod ordered the slaughter of boy babies. We cringe at that. Today boy and girl babies are murdered before birth in figures that run into millions, but the average individual never even raises an eyebrow.

Ruth Graham said that if God does not punish America in judgment He will have to apologize to Sodom and Gomorrah. American pride boasts that destruction won't happen here, but history is one long record of nations that made that same boast, and now we see only the Pyramids, the Parthenon, and the Colosseum.

Unless there is soon a genuine turning to God in America we may end up in the biggest buzzard roost of all time.

34 "All Live Unto Him"

Some of the Pharisees came to Jesus with a question about the status of marriage in the life to come (Luke 20:27–38). In Jesus' answer He made the statement that God is not a God of the dead but of the living: "For all live unto him" (Luke 20:38).

No one who has ever lived has ceased to exist. Everyone is somewhere. No one dies unto God. Our brains reel at the thought, but we believe that in this natural world nothing really goes out of existence. Burn a log and some of it goes up in smoke, some remains in ashes, but nothing really goes out into nothingness.

Human personality is a precious commodity, and anyone God gave breath to is too valuable to disappear utterly. Of course that is a lot of people, but God has limitless space in His roomy universe. All Christians have eternal life, but the Scriptures do not suggest that countless unsaved souls are annihilated.

We must distinguish between our bodies and the persons who inhabit those bodies. Our eyes do not see; we see with our eyes. So with hearing and feeling. We must distinguish between tenant and tenement. The old body disintegrates in the grave, but whoever went about in that body and used it does not go "ashes to ashes and dust to dust." None die unto God!

35 At Christmas Time

I have a tiny musical Christmas tree with a wee angel in it that plays "Standing on the Promises." When I wind it up it chimes with valiant enthusiasm, but as it runs down it also slows down, sometimes stopping before the tune is finished—that is, it stops standing on the promises and is only sitting on the premises! I have often preached about how Christians mistake the one for the other!

It is possible to stand on the promises in an austere orthodoxy that knows little of resting in the promises and living day by day on the strength of them. I want to stand on the promises and not run down in the middle of my life like the little music box.

36 The Missing Love

Twice in his Epistles Paul speaks of lost humanity and the people of the last days as being "without natural affection." Frightful statistics reveal millions who cannot get along with each other in marriage. I believe that most of that multitude are without natural affection, knowing nothing of natural human affection, and of course utterly unconscious of Divine love.

Old-fashioned sweetheart love is an unknown experience with most mortals today, and many of our youth and many more oldsters know only physical attraction. They meet each other pretty much like two dogs getting acquainted down the street. Listen to the love songs we hear today (if songs they be) and hark back to "Moonlight and Roses," "I Love You Truly," and others of that kind, and you know what I mean. We are a generation of mere bodies with addled brains, incapable of the affection that held our fathers and mothers through trials and tribulation into a ripe old age. There are exceptions that prove the rule, thank God, but one wonders whether there are enough of them to hold humanity together much longer in the flood of humanism and anarchy.

I am speaking now, of course, only about human love and not the love of God that moves the Spirit-filled Christian. We can know nothing of that except by the new birth from above. But even ordinary human affection has a place in ordinary morality, and when that goes, the structure of old Adam at his best collapses.

37 Mr. Fearing

John Bunyan never painted with greater skill a common human type when he gave us Mr. Fearing in *Pilgrim's Progress*. This dear soul lived all his days afraid that he would never reach heaven but made it anyway. Maclaren says, "There are none so far away from false confidence (as to this salvation) as those who tremble lest they may be cherishing it. They manage to distill for themselves bitter vinegar of self-accusation out of grand words in the Bible meant to afford them the wine of gladness and consolation."

When Mr. Fearing reached the great river of Death he almost panicked. But the water had never been so low as it was that day and he got across not much above wetshod!

We have no reason to doubt or be timid about anything as sure as the salvation of our souls. But we are not all geared up alike and many have pillowed their faint hearts on the dear lines:

> "When I tread the verge of Jordan,
> Bid my anxious fears subside!"

Satan, the accuser of the saints, takes great delight in worrying feeble believers who sigh when they should be singing. But when these people peruse the pages of God's Word, they will find that they are in company with David, Jeremiah, and Paul, who were sometimes tortured with fears and fightings without and within.

We may not always see the lifted-up Savior as we wish we might, but we can look when we cannot see, and we are saved by the direction of our looking, not the clearness of what we sometimes see. Jesus only said, "Look," and if we look and keep walking the way we are looking we will cross the river saying with Mr. Fearing, "I shall, I shall!"

38 Motto on the Wall

I hung a section from an old calendar on my bedroom wall. It reads, "The LORD will perfect that which concerneth me" (Ps. 138:8). At night when the lights are out I can see the motto, and though it is too dark to read it, I know what it says. Sometimes I lie awake pondering my past, present, and future. At eighty-one years I review a long span of years. An old saint advised, "forefancy your deathbed." There is nothing morbid about that. I marvel that we mortals give so little thought to eternity when we live on the brink of it all the time!

My motto is a promise of God. It says that He is Lord of the hitherto and the henceforth and that my times are in His hand. It does not always look like it. Doubts and fears often beset me. Who will take care of me if I get sick? Suppose my invitations to preach should stop coming? I have no organization, no business setup, not even a secretary. What if the doors would close? Then I look at my motto on the wall. God has not failed me since I started preaching in 1913. It says God will perfect that which concerns me. He who has begun a good work in me will see it through. I hope for a good finish, a home run in the last inning, but things may happen that do not seem to be part of the pattern. I cannot fit some of them into my jigsaw puzzle. But He is faithful who promised.

It is more than a motto that hangs on the wall. It is a check from the bank of heaven with the signature of God. Thief cannot steal nor rust corrupt what I have deposited there. It is the one and only safe and sure investment.

39 When We Don't Know What to Do

I have been facing a decision lately. I have no "druthers" about it and am willing to go either way. All I can do is make a decision after I ask God, in faith, for wisdom, nothing wavering, for a wavering man is like a wave of the sea driven and tossed by the wind.

Times of decision are no light matter and we are often hard pressed in spirit. It is true that Jesus said, "Let not your heart be troubled" (John 14:1, 27), but He also said at another time, "Now is my soul troubled; and what shall I say? (John 12:27). But He followed that with, "Father, glorify thy name." The thing to say in every situation is, "Thy will be done, glorify Thy name."

When we face a difficult decision, let us make sure we have spread the whole issue out before God without reservation and are willing to go any way that is His way. Then we may ask for His wisdom and believe that we have the answer. Whatsoever things we desire when we pray we must believe that we receive them and we shall have them (Mark 11:24). Dr. R. A. Torrey was troubled about the grammar of that verse for a while . . . "Believe you have it and you will have it," but he decided to quit worrying about the grammar and started trusting the Word!

In no other way can we have peace and assurance than to accept God's will, pray, then trust we have the answer. The flesh and the devil will try to disturb our souls until we live continually in mere hope instead of certainty. We must remember Jesus' example. He came to die for our sins on the cross—a mission that meant suffering beyond imagination. There was a momentary human reaction, during which He sweated profusely, like great drops of blood, but He did purchase our salvation. When we don't know what to do we do know what to say: "Father, glorify Thy name."

40 A Sweet Little Girl

As I strolled along my favorite trail I saw a sweet little girl vigorously pedaling her bike my way. She passed me with a cheery "Hi!" and "Excuse me!" and then was gone. As I watched her disappear I surmised, "That youngster has been brought up right. I'd like to meet her dad and mother!"

That little girl will never know how much sunlight she brought into my drab morning. Some time ago a newspaper asked, "What became of the magic of childhood?" Today our children are fast becoming a generation of computer whiz kids before they reach their teens. They seem like miniature adults.

Our Savior said, "Except ye be converted, and become as little children, ye shall not enter into the kingdom of heaven" (Matt. 18:3). How will we ever fit that into the modern jargon?

I pray God that sweet little girl will be spared the tragedy and heartbreak and disaster of thousands just as sweet, but who are now the scum of the earth. Yet I must say that today I have the best response ever from youth. In recent services they have walked down a church aisle on a clear and hard challenge to know and follow Christ as Paul wished to know Him and the power of His resurrection, the fellowship of His sufferings and conformity to His death.

God bless that sweet little girl who made my morning on the trail so bright!

41 Two Ways to Leave Church

"He hath filled the hungry with good things; and the rich he hath sent empty away" (Luke 1:53).

Have you ever watched a congregation leave church on Sunday? Some came for a blessing and were not disappointed. Some came for nothing and with nothing they went away. There is old Sister Jones. She came with a heart hungry for more of God and she goes away happy. There is Deacon Bigshot. He is rich and increased with goods and has need of nothing, and with nothing he departs. You get what you come for.

We major nowadays on relevance and minor on reverence. We ought to go to worship as though it were the first time, as though it might be the best time, and as though it could be the last time. Let a Sunday crowd arrive at church in that frame and there will be a revival! They will not come out murmuring a weak "I enjoyed the sermon," but praising God.

Mary's words in the Magnificat uttered the rejoicing of her heart that God had chosen a plain maiden of the common people to be the Messiah's mother. It is in line with the way God always operates in passing up the wise, mighty, and noble, and revealing Himself to babes. He satisfies the hungry heart with good things but the rich He sends away empty.

If we could get an honest report on the real reason why most people went to the average church last Sunday we would understand why nothing happened. There were too few thirsty hearts and too many Laodiceans, increased with goods and needing nothing. They got what they came for.

42 "Go, Tell That Fox"

When the Pharisees tried to frighten our Lord with a threat from Herod our Lord gave an amazing answer, found only in Luke. He said in effect, "I have a life work to do and a ministry to perform and I will complete it" (Luke 13:32). When man sets out to do the will of God he will hear from the Pharisees and the "foxes," to use our Lord's word for Herod, who intends to divert and destroy it. But this passage is just another way of saying that when we are in God's work and will we are immortal until our work is done.

When the Pharisees and the foxes try to confuse and discourage us with their predictions and warnings, let us tell them we are on God's schedule and He who has begun a good work in us will finish it. The man who has set out to do the will of God in his life is linked up with heaven, and nothing that happens on earth can defeat him unless he himself departs from what God called him to do and be.

Jesus was often saying, "My time is not yet come." Then on the night of His arrest in the Garden of Gethsemane He said, "This is *your* hour, and the power of darkness" (Luke 22:53, italics mine). His hour and the Jewish leaders' hour met in a head-on collision. It looked like Jesus lost, but He won through death and resurrection. Whoever lives for Christ is immortal; he lives until his work is finished on earth, and he then continues life in heaven.

43 Getting Used to It

A secular publication makes this important observation: "The desensitization of twentieth-century man is more than a danger to the common safety. There are some things we have no right ever to get to."

Christians today are getting used to the dark. We are up against the power that controls this dark world, against spiritual agents from the very headquarters of evil. There is a slow, subtle, sinister brainwashing process gradually desensitizing us to evil. Little by little sin is made to appear less sinful. We are being homogenized, absorbed, assimilated into this age. We accept its literature, its music, its art, its language, without inner or outer protest although we are told to hate evil, abhor evil, abstain from the very appearance of evil. Soon things do not appear to be so dark as we grow accustomed to them. It is not that our minds are broadening but that our consciences are stretching! We live in peaceful coexistence with the world, the flesh, and the devil.

Christians are also getting used to the light. Jesus said that His home town, Capernaum, would fare worse at the judgment than Sodom and Gomorrah. He had moved to Capernaum to fulfill the Scripture, "The people that walked in darkness have seen a great light; they that dwell in the land of the shadow of death, upon them hath the light shined" (Isa. 9:2). That light did not come to Sodom and Gomorrah. Capernaum took that light for granted. There is a comfortable attitude about Jesus Christ in our churches today, and it is our greatest peril. After all, we are not judged so much by how many sins we have committed but by how much light we have rejected. We bemoan the Sodomites today and well we may, but we had better be more concerned for Capernaumites in our churches who would never harm Jesus but are so used to Him that they ignore Him.

Darkness and light are opposites, and we ought never get used to either!

44 Prison Birds at Midnight

Midnight in prison is hardly the best setup for gospel singing, but Paul and Silas turned a prison into a pulpit and the other prisoners heard them. Some might have suggested to these flaming evangelists that sleeping prisoners should not be disturbed at such an hour ("Let all things be done decently and in order" [1 Cor. 14:40].), but Paul had his priorities straight and his program was not planned by ordinary procedure but by the Spirit of God. In time past the devil had inflamed Saul of Tarsus with such hatred of Christ and His church that Saul exhaled it like his very breath. Now the new Paul was inflamed by the fire of God's Spirit to start a commotion wherever he went, turning the world upside down. This time it landed him and Silas in jail, and at midnight, of all times, they started a song service.

Today the world and even the professing church are anxious to avoid disturbance and keep everything quiet. Consequently there are not many incidents like the earthquake that freed the prisoners and brought the jailer to his knees in conviction crying, "What must I do to be saved?"

When the early church got into trouble with government officials they were rebuked for their boldness, but instead of toning down they prayed for more boldness—the very thing that got them into trouble to begin with! The kind of Christianity that can sing in prison at midnight will always be heard by prisoners of sin in this awful world, and God will set His approval on it by setting them free.

45 Birds and Buses

I am in Knoxville as I write this chapter. I am preaching in a church each evening and enjoying walks during the wonderful May mornings.

I discovered a little hill here fairly well removed from the maddening crowd's ignoble strife. I slip out to that spot and listen to the meadowlark and the indigo bunting. Across from the hill at a distance runs a wide highway, and the noise is deafening. If Gabriel blew his trumpet we would never hear him! I am thankful for this little hill and for the birds. It is difficult to escape the bedlam of these days, and it grows worse all the while.

If we do not soon raise up some prophets who know solitude and soul-searching—children of Issachar who have understanding of the times to know what Israel ought to do—we are done for. If we do not learn to break away from the din of this present drunken, drugged, diseased, demonized culture, come apart and be still, we will end up a generation of nonentities, numbers, sheep led to the slaughter.

I read of a factory worker, a poor man who labored all day in the profanity and putridity of godless co-workers. Every evening he got away from the machines that were making him into a robot to climb a little hill nearby. When asked why he did it, he said, "I must keep reminding myself that I have a soul!"

Any escape you may devise to defeat the devil and break the vicious circle of modern living is worth trying. By all means take time to be holy and avoid the madness that gains the world at the soul's expense. No wealth, no success, no earthly rewards are worth that price. Do not lose the world of the birds in the world of the buses! Find a little hill far from the traffic of "progress" while you still have a soul!

46 "Tentative" and "Terminal"

"This is a *tentative* appointment." "This is only a *tentative* plan." We use the word when arrangements are temporary and uncertain. But, come to think of it, don't we operate most of the time on a tentative basis? Life is so unpredictable, so little is sure. The best-laid plans of mice and men are never for certain. No wonder the Bible tells us to make our remarks low-key when we talk about what we plan to do tomorrow.

Another uncertain word is "terminal." We call some cancer victim nearing death a terminal case. Aren't we all? I don't want you to lay down this piece feeling worse than when you started reading it, but you are a terminal case. We must all call it a day and depart unless Jesus returns before long and changes our plans.

"Tentative" and "terminal," that is the essence of temporality. And yet we are eternal, for somewhere we shall continue. Nobody is terminated in God's sight—"all live unto him." We never cease to exist. Put eternality into your head and heart. The real you, the tenant within your tenement, will live on somewhere. The choice of residence is yours.

47 The Ancient Sacrifice

The young Christian who starts reading through the Bible for the first time may get along fine through Genesis and most of Exodus but mire in the chapters about the building of the Tabernacle and the garb of the priests and the many details of duties under the Mosaic law. He is tempted to give up unless he learns that God has recorded all these facts and figures for the information of Israel in her new day nationally in the age to come.

The Christian who is not under the law is likely to pass over this heavy reading and leave it to antiquity, but he should not be in a hurry. The temple is now the human heart and we are under grace, but we may overlook one tremendous fact. God places high value on holiness, reverence, and worship. Our Lord came to earth when the law was still taught, but He did not brush it aside. It has been fulfilled in Him, and He approved neither idol worship or idle worship but ideal worship in Spirit and truth.

God wants His worshipers whether long ago or today to come to Him in sanctified reverence, with a broken and contrite heart. When one considers the way most church goers go to worship today, he shudders at the casual approach of a generation to whom "holy" and "holiness" mean nothing. One must prepare to hear a sermon just as another must prepare the sermon. We no longer offer animal sacrifices or observe rituals, but it is still as true as ever that

> "The tumult and the shouting dies;
> The captains and the kings depart;
> Still stands Thine ancient sacrifice—
> A broken and a contrite heart."

48 "Only Believe"

When the father of a demon-possessed boy brought his son to Jesus, he said, "If thou canst do any thing. ..." Jesus replied, "If thou canst believe" (Mark 9:22, 23). There are no "ifs" about what God can do. The "if" is with us. Anything is possible within the limits of God's Word and God's will, our need and our faith. Believing God is not religious auto-suggestion. It is not the flesh engaged in positive thinking. It is the Christian, the one in whom Christ lives, taking God at His Word.

God's Word and will, our need and our faith do impose certain restrictions. We often want what we do not need. God did not remove Paul's thorn in the flesh but He did something better, perfecting His strength in Paul's weakness. Within these limitations there are blessings innumerable if we only believe.

Chanting, "I believe," does not guarantee results as though we had a magic password. Exploring God's Word we will discover blessings we did not know were in His will. And we need some intensive investigation of what we really need. There are rich people riding around in limousines who have never found out what they really need. And there are sickly Christians living on crackers and cheese when they have a standing invitation to the feast of the grace of God. What a shake-up in status there is when we find out what is ours now in Christ Jesus!

Positive thinking will not do it unless we balance it with some good negative thinking that says "no" to the devil while it says "yes" to God. To put on the Lord Jesus and make no provision for the flesh is a good sample of true positive-negative thinking. "Only believe" depends on whom you believe and why.

49 Between Two Fires

At our Lord's trial Peter warmed himself by the fire in the courtyard. A Christian is always on dangerous ground when he warms himself by the devil's fire, following at a distance and soon to deny his Lord. Here Peter became a backslider, still a believer but not a disciple (the angel at the sepulcher said, "Go tell his disciples and Peter ..." [Luke 16:7]).

At another fire, kindled on the Tiberias beach, Peter was restored to fellowship. Between those two fires were hours of anguish for this broken-hearted man. Living between two such fires is poor business and neither fire will warm you. The devil always arranges to have a blaze convenient for Christians who are already following Jesus afar off. It is tantalizing on chilly nights when the Adversary is getting ready to crucify the Savior afresh and put Him to open shame. To a Christian found where he does not belong, it will mean grief and tears. If persisted in he will become a hardened backslider and hard to reclaim.

An alarming percentage of church members today are quite comfortably warming at the wrong fire. The rooster's crowing that once brought conviction no longer disturbs them. If they have ever been saved they are no longer in fellowship, and if they have never been anything but church members there has never been any fellowship with the Lord. To win these two kinds of people today is a major task. They so outnumber the faithful that true Christians cannot get to the goal for stumbling over their own team members. They furnish their own greatest interference!

Are you living between two fires? If your spirit is broken Christ will ask, "Do you love me?" and your heart will cry, "Thou knowest I love thee." Then He will say, "Feed my sheep." But He will say more. He said to Peter, "You once went where you pleased but now you will have to go where you do not want to go. And don't worry about what happens to John. Follow me yourself!"

50 Too Much

I have written elsewhere about a week's stay near a major highway with its deafening roar of traffic in Knoxville. I said that I hoped Gabriel wouldn't blow his trumpet near such a pandemonium because we might not hear him. Now as I write, I am near Seattle and the story is the same. I watch the pell-mell rush from Dan to Beersheba and say to myself, "I don't believe God ever intended that we mortals should live at such a pace." This hastening host rarely stops long enough to think about God's intent for their lives. They go like sheep to the slaughter.

Human minds and bodies are not geared for this stressful kind of living. The price exacted from both mind and body is hideous. And somehow this crazy life pattern gets itself called progress! Lost in his skyscrapers, zooming through the sky in his jets, boasting of technical marvels and brain-boggling gadgets, man never stops long enough to enquire, "What is all this about?"

I am not trying to call us back to the good old days—that weren't really so good—to dirt roads, horse-and-buggy transportation, and kerosene lamps. But we have gone overboard, throwing out the baby with the bathwater and are the victims of our own inventiveness.

It's too much.

51 The Prevenient Angel

"Who shall roll us away the stone from the door of the sepulchre?" (Mark 16:3).

Jesus had said He would rise on the third day, but here heartbroken women had come seeking the living among the dead. Like thousands of His disciples to this day they crossed the bridge before they reached it. They did not count on divine intervention and expected no angels. The grave had been secured by stone, seal, and soldiers. A heavenly visitor who not only rolled the stone away but sat on it in heavenly triumph may have seemed possible in their remotest thinking but not probable.

How often in my pitiful doubts and fears have I met the inevitable in my nervous dread and never counted on the prevenient angel. Then when I reached the spot I had dreaded I was shamed again at the pitiful failure of my faith and could hear Jesus' "O ye of little faith, how long will it be ere ye believe me?"

As a boy I used to look at the familiar picture of the guardian angel standing with a little child at the edge of a cliff. Theoretically and theologically I believed in heavenly helpers who minister to the heirs of salvation, but when a crisis arose my hopes of their intervention were slim. But now with the long look back over eight decades I know that I was often attended by prevenient angels though I knew them not. They arrived at my place of danger before I did. Stones and seals and soldiers mean nothing when a mighty angel comes down to roll the stone away.

52 The Revival–Evangelism Mix-up

On the matter of revival and evangelism the church today has begun in the Spirit but is now, sadly, trying to perfect herself in the flesh. Dr. Martyn Lloyd-Jones has said: "I am convinced that nothing can avail but churches and ministers on their knees in total dependence on God. As long as you go on organizing, people will not fall on their knees and implore God to come and heal them." Today great churches have been filled with a host of members without a personal experience of Christ and others who may be believers but know next to nothing about the Holy Spirit. These people can be aroused into religious activity in the flesh, even doing personal visitation and contributing heavily to church work, compassing sea and land to make more proselytes. The process, that started with Constantine paganizing Christianity instead of Christianizing paganism, has filled churches with unconverted prospects until the biggest evangelistic field is the average Sunday morning congregation. We cannot get to the goal because we furnish our own greatest interference and stumble over our own team!

Such a Sunday morning approach does not meet with the favor of some ministers because it would be a bombshell to call some of our "best" members to repentance. True revival begins within the church calling Christians to a new life in the Spirit, but it also means converting thousands of present members for the first time to a new birth by the Spirit. That is a stupendous task considering the way things are today and involves far more than popular meetings, happy singing, and canvassing new "prospects."

53 Bringing Back the King

Nothing has confused the work of the church more than misunderstanding the difference between bringing in Christ's kingdom and bringing back Christ, the King. The Scriptures do not set forth the conversion of all humanity or the Christianization of this age. Jesus said, "When the Son of man cometh, shall He find faith on the earth?" (Luke 18:8). He said the time before His return will be as in the days of Lot. Paul pictures the end times as marked by love of money, moral corruption, and departure from the truth.

We read that the days of Lot were spent in eating and drinking, marrying and giving in marriage, buying and selling, planting and building. In their proper place these things are not evil, but when they are all we live for to the denial of God, then we are as worldly as a young blade on a dance floor at two o'clock in the morning. Certainly this is the lifestyle of today, and to let this age be the pattern and style of our living is worldliness.

The professing church by and large has joined the world and the world is joining the church to become Babylon in the last sad chapter of earth's story. But God is taking out a people for Himself and that is the true church. We may not be able at times to say just who is who but God knows His own. Some religionists become so infatuated with the world church that they show little concern about the coming King.

Dr. James M. Gray summed it up well:

> "Why say ye not a word of bringing back the King?
> Why sing ye not of Jesus and His reign?
> Why tell ye of the Kingdom and of its glories sing,
> But nothing of His coming back again?"

54 Lord of the Leftovers

After Jesus fed the multitude He said, "Gather up the fragments that remain, that nothing be lost" (John 6:12). Our Lord is not stingy; He gives liberally. But neither is He wasteful. He had a purpose for the basketsful that remained.

Often I preach to people who have wasted their early years and should have been preachers or missionaries. I meet late beginners in the ministry who start in their forties and sometimes excel early beginners because their time is short and they buckle down to work in dead earnest.

Some of you who may read these lines have lost many years but there still remain some baskets of leftovers. All is not lost. Some decide to quit when there remains much land to be possessed and much work to be done. Do not decide that you have had it. You may make a home run in the last inning, win the race on the last lap. Some of the Geritol crowd may still be going when many of the Pepsi generation have died.

> "Lord of the years that are left to me,
> I give them to Thy hand.
> Take me and make me and mold me
> To the pattern Thou hast planned."

55 No More Sea

"And there was no more sea" (Rev. 21:1).

The last book in the Bible was written by a lonely old preacher on a desolate island surrounded by a surging sea. John, the last of the apostles, was in exile on Patmos for "the word of God and . . . the testimony of Jesus Christ" (1:2). All the other apostles were now with the Lord. John might well have asked, "Is this what I get for being a soldier of the cross, a follower of the Lamb?" It looked like persecution but it was really promotion, for God pulled back the curtain and revealed history's greatest vision of the future. It was worth exile on Patmos to see that!

The vision reached its climax when John beheld a new heaven and a new earth. We read, "For the first heaven and the first earth were passed away; and there was no more sea" (21:1). Why are we given this strange extra information that there was no more sea?

There is a lot of ocean in the Book of Revelation. One hears the roar of the waves all the way through the Apocalypse. One reads about a sea of glass mingled with fire. The star called Wormwood fell upon the sea. The beast arose out of the sea. The great angel threw a mighty stone into the sea. And when at last John saw the new heaven and the new earth, the sea he was so tired of had disappeared.

What does it mean? For one thing, the sea is a symbol of mystery. "Thy way is in the sea, and thy path in the great waters, and thy footsteps are not known" (Ps. 77:19). "Thy judgments are a mighty deep" (Ps. 36:6). "O the depth of the riches both of the wisdom and knowledge of God! how unsearchable are his judgments, and his ways past finding out!" (Rom. 11:33).

Remember that the Jew was not a sailor. He was a landlubber, not a seafarer. When he started out from Egypt for the Promised Land, the first thing that got in his way

65

was a sea. There are no seas in Israel. The Sea of Galilee is only a lake. To the Jew, the ocean stood for awesome mystery and awful misery. He preferred green pastures and still waters. And after all the centuries, not only to the Jew but to all the rest of us, the ocean is still not something ordinary and commonplace that we take as a matter of course. In spite of how much we have traveled it, explored it, studied it, and written about it, the sea awes us.

What would we find if we could drain the sea dry? What continents would show up, what canyons and craters, mountains and valleys? Think of the dead that lie in it, the sunken ships entombed in it, the wealth lost in it, the power hidden in it! It is a world of mystery that surrounds us.

The sea is a symbol of the mystery we call life. We are so ignorant, we know so little, only a little tip of the iceberg rises above the surface. We still see through a glass darkly and know in part. But one day the mystery will clear and there will be no more sea.

The sea is also a symbol of evil. It symbolizes not only mystery but misery. "The wicked are like the troubled sea . . . whose waters cast up mire and dirt" (Isa. 57:20). We live in an ocean of evil. Arnold Toynbee pondered long why a nation as literate as Germany could be deceived by a maniac like Hitler. He concluded that there must be a vein of original sin in human nature everywhere, that civilization is a thin cake of custom overlying a molten mass of wickedness that is always boiling up for an opportunity to burst out.

Well did song writer H. L. Gilmour express it:

> "My soul in sad exile was out on life's sea,
> So burdened with sin and distress"

He went on to say,

> "I've anchored my soul in the 'Haven of Rest,'
> I'll sail the wide seas no more;
> The tempest may sweep o'er the wild, stormy deep;
> In Jesus I'm safe evermore."

The devil stirred up a storm on the Sea of Galilee while our Lord slept in the boat. He stirred up a tempest called Euroclydon when Paul was on his voyage toward Rome. We live on a tempestuous ocean of iniquity but we look for a new heaven and new earth where righteousness dwells and where there shall be no more sea.

But Isaiah 57:20 says more: "The wicked are like the troubled sea, when it cannot rest." The sea is a symbol of unrest. This world has never been so restless as it is now. Tranquilizers sell at a record high. Mental hospitals are crowded. Abuse of drugs and alcohol and immorality are causing more and more people to say, "There is no peace." Never has a generation invented so many devices and spent so much money to make itself comfortable and never has there been such an unhappy generation. They have tried all sorts of ways to find peace but have failed to find the only solution—faith in Jesus Christ. God's map of the new heaven and new earth does not show any oceans of sin and unrest.

More than anything else, the sea is a symbol of separation. How lonely John must have been on Patmos! Gone were all the other apostles. Gone was the fellowship of the church and all his Christian friends. No matter which way he looked—north, south, east, west—there was only ocean. How he longed for a day when there would be no more sea! You and I are exiles on this earth separated from the saints of centuries past. We can only read about them or what they wrote. And we are separated from the saints of our own day who have gone to be with the Lord. Of course we greatly miss our close friends and loved ones.

But the day is coming when there will be no more sea. William Jennings Bryan said, "Life is a narrow strip between the companionship of yesterday and the reunion of tomorrow." Above all reunion with earth's dear ones is the prospect of seeing Him whom, though now we see Him not, we love.

> "When my life-work is ended and I cross the swelling tide,
> When the bright and glorious morning I shall see,
> I shall know my Redeemer when I reach the other side,
> And His smile will be the first to welcome me."

56 The Seventh Dip

Naaman was an able captain in the Syrian army, in good standing with King Ben-hadad, but he was a leper. When he took off his decorations at night and looked at his decaying body, his military glory departed. He came to Elisha to be healed and that man of God did not even come out to meet him but simply commanded, "Go and wash in Jordan seven times" (2 Kings 5:10). Naaman lost his temper, "Dip in Jordan, that dirty creek! We have Abana and Pharpar in Syria!" (cf. v. 12). His companions persuaded him to give it a try, but when he had gone down and up six times there was no sign of a miracle. They might have begun to wonder whether their captain had been "taken" by a false prophet. But on the seventh dip Naaman's flesh became as the flesh of a child!

The miracle happened at the end of complete obedience. If the blind man sent by Jesus to the pool of Siloam, his eyes covered with mud, had not felt his way down the street in simple obedience, he would have died a blind man. John McNeill preached about this incident and shouted to his congregation, "Aye, and some of you have had the mud applied again and again, you have heard sermon after sermon, but you've never done the next thing and you're blinder than you ever were before!" Faith must be followed by obedience.

Philip, the evangelist, fresh out of great meetings in Samaria, might have seen no point in walking a desert road, but there was a eunuch down that road who needed to be saved. Complete obedience brought the miracle! When God bids you dip in Jordan, wash in Siloam, or walk a desert trail, the victory lies at the end of that venture. When God says, "Go!" that is not a suggestion but a command!

57 Don't Pitch Toward Sodom!

Lot did not move lock, stock, and barrel into the middle of Sodom, but he headed that way. We read that the men of Sodom were wicked and sinned before the Lord continually. Lot was a righteous man and was vexed by the lifestyle of Sodom. He was put on the city council and he prospered financially, but he had to flee for his life when judgment fell. Finally he died in disgrace. That is too high a price to pay to live in Sodom.

Jesus said that before He returns the situation on earth will be as in the days of Lot. They ate and drank, married and were given in marriage, bought and sold, planted and built. All of that has its proper place, but when God is not honored it is worldliness.

Too many Christians pitch their tents toward Sodom. It is the direction of their lives. But we are meant to be pilgrims and strangers, looking for a city with foundations whose builder and maker is God. Which way are you "pitched"? If you are pitched toward Sodom, give a little time and Sodom will be your permanent address. You might make city council, but Sodom is destined for destruction. Better flee while you can!

58 The Attending Impediment

In his immortal *Pilgrim's Progress* Bunyan tells us about Christian making his difficult way through the Valley of the Shadow of Death. He heard a voice saying, "I will fear no evil, for Thou art with me." Christian reasoned, "If God be with him, why not with me?" Then he added, "Though by reason of the impediment that attends this place, I cannot perceive it."

Nothing is scarcer today in Christians and churches than a sense of the presence of God. Moses asked, "How shall we know that we are thy people? Is it not in that thou goest with us?" The devil will do anything to destroy the awareness of God's presence. One of his favorite tools is annoying circumstances. Old Bud Robinson was holding meetings in a spiritually barren church. He was staying with the pastor, and one evening he was in his room praying loudly enough to be heard a mile away. The pastor looked in and said to Bud, "Dear Brother, God is not deaf." Bud replied, "I know He's not, but he's a long way from this place!" Evidently there was an attending impediment that shut out a sense of God.

How often is church service accompanied by a spirit of infirmity, coldness, irreverence, and worldliness that squelches the moving of the Spirit of God! A dear brother, active in a great church, said as we talked about the many activities going on, "But we lack something. I suppose it is the Holy Spirit." He was conscious of an "attending impediment" that nullified most of the church work going on.

The answer to the world, the flesh, and the devil saying, "God is nowhere" is the affirmation that God is now here. The awareness of His presence makes the difference.

Darkness cannot be shoveled out of a room, but we can turn on the light. Joel bemoaned the day when the heathen asked, "Where is now your God?" God is still here among us, but we must deal firmly with the impediments that cloud His presence. Otherwise we cannot perceive Him.

59 From Limp to Leap

The healing of the lame man as recorded in Acts 3 holds precious lessons for us all.

First, let's look at the lameness. The human race is a race of cripples, maimed in body, mind, and spirit. Even those who seem, apart from saving grace, to be hale and hearty are best described by Isaiah as without soundness but with wounds and bruises and putrefying sores. Sin is a grievous affliction, and we are lame in our souls from birth to death unless we are born again. The crutches are not always visible, and sick souls try to laugh sin off, drink it off, pretend its non-existence, but God knows about it and so do we in better moments.

Peter and John bade the lame man, "Look on us" (v. 4). Deliverance lay in a look. Peter and John were not magnifying themselves; with them stood One whom the lame man and the onlookers couldn't see. There stood one among them whom they knew not. Any Christian and especially any gospel preacher filled with the Spirit may well say to the lame, "Look on us. We are nothing of ourselves but there stands with us One, who, through faith in His name, can make you whole."

Peter took the lame man by the hand and lifted him up. The look was followed by the lift. There is plenty of uplifting these days, but much of it is old Adam trying to lift old Adam. The true Christian, filled with the Spirit of the living Christ has life in his lift. It was so with this man and he leaped. He may have come limping but he went away leaping. No wonder we sing:

> "Hear Him, ye deaf; His praise ye dumb,
> Your loosened tongues employ;
> Ye blind, behold your Saviour come,
> And leap, ye lame, for joy!"

60 Praying "Accordingly"

An accordionist is one who plays an accordion. A praying Christian should be an "accordingist," praying by the "accordings" of God that underlie successful praying.

We must pray according to His Word. The man who prays Scripturally prays successfully. We must pray according to His will (1 John 5:14, 15). We must pray according to our need (Phil. 4:19). We do not always want what we need or need what we want. And we must pray according to our faith. Several times Jesus said, "According to your faith be it unto you."

Paul's thorn in the flesh was not removed, but he received a greater blessing. Sometimes God gives us extra blessings just as a loving father gives to his child something he wanted although he may not have needed it. "Ye have not because ye ask not." And even when faith is weak God may move a mountain and surprise us. God is not stingy, He giveth liberally and upbraideth not. Even when faith is low and we can only say, "Lord, I believe, help thou mine unbelief," He may work a miracle. And often we may need to learn "the patience of unanswered prayer."

Recognizing these four *accordings* before you start praying. Remember, it might be disastrous if you received everything you thought you needed! Paul found out that greater than a trip to the third heaven or the joy of deliverance from a thorn in the flesh, is to know that God's grace is always sufficient, that we are strong when we are weak and His strength is made perfect through weakness. That is the Christian's greatest experience.